TEACHERS ROCK

JOURNAL

THIS JOURNAL BELONGS TO:

____

____

____

MW00930661

Made in the USA
Coppell, TX
06 May 2024

32088346R00066